Cracked Pots

Christie McFadden

ISBN 978-1-63961-358-8 (paperback)
ISBN 978-1-63961-359-5 (digital)

Christian Faith Publishing, Inc.
832 Park Avenue
Meadville, PA 16335
www.christianfaithpublishing.com

Printed in the United States of America

Contents

A million thoughts go through your head daily while riding an emotional roller coaster. Good, bad, helpful, hurtful, and even destructive.

It's the forever battle of good and evil for your soul. No matter how strong your faith and love for God is, Satan is always there to turn you away from God.

> The thief comes only to steal and kill and destroy; I have come that they may have life, and have it to the full. (John 10:10 NIV)

Satan comes to destroy God's work in you, but Jesus came to destroy Satan's work.

By removing and taking control of the junk in your head, you can have control over your life. You can have control over your thoughts and remove all the negativity that consumes you. Recognize the cause(s) of the mess in your life, and find a way to limit or remove it (or them).

Every time you have a nagging thought, say, "Satan, leave me alone, and I don't need you in my life." Ask God to remove Satan and the reoccurring thoughts that linger day in and day out.

Pray daily for God to give you the tools to get your thoughts and feelings under control and to bring balance, purpose, and success to your life. You are designed by God for a purpose.

What reoccurring thoughts consume you daily?

_____

_____

_____

_____

_____

Notes

_____

_____

_____

_____

_____

_____

_____

_____

Write a Prayer

_____

_____

_____

_____

_____

_____

_____

_____

Self-Esteem/Doubt

Merriam-Webster defines *self-esteem* as "a confidence and satisfaction in oneself." Doubt is "a lack of confidence."

Celebrate yourself daily. Set small, achievable goals; then accomplish them as a way to believe in yourself again. Give yourself enough time to realistically achieve the goals. Each day provides an opportunity to choose how we live our lives. The Holy Spirit is the only one who can change you from the inside out.

> Teaching them to observe all things that I have commanded you; and lo, I am with you always, even to the end of the age. Amen. (Matthew 28:20 NKJV)

Write Proverbs 30:5.

_____
_____
_____
_____
_____

Pray and reflect on the real you whom God has created.

_____
_____
_____
_____
_____

Everyone's struggles may be different, but the rescue is the same. Your hope, identity, and security rest only in the Savior, in what He did for us on the cross and through His resurrection, and in whom He says we are as a new creation.

You can be the best version of yourself when you take care of yourself. Love yourself enough to say "no" to take care of yourself. Getting healthy leads to a better relationship with God, which, in turn, improves your relationship with others.

Surround yourself with positive people who will support, encourage, and challenge you in good ways. Toxic people will bring you down, drain your energy, and make you feel bad.

Notes

_____

_____

_____

_____

_____

_____

_____

_____

_____

What can you do to be healthier?

_____

_____

_____

_____

_____

What are you proud of yourself for doing?

Today?

_____
_____
_____
_____
_____

This week?

_____
_____
_____
_____
_____

This month?

_____
_____
_____
_____
_____

Everyone is flawed. Now stop and think about that for a minute. *Everyone* on this earth is flawed.

How are you flawed?

_____
_____
_____
_____
_____

Never doubt the power of God. Let God manage your emotional health.

Now write a prayer, and give God all your negative thoughts and words.

_____

_____

_____

_____

_____

Control your emotions to believe the truth. Often, a person will knowingly allow themselves to believe a lie because of fear or self-pity. Believers must commit to truth regardless of the repercussions, turning negatives into positives, weaknesses into strengths, and tragedies into triumphs. Look for opportunities for God to be glorified.

The Bible makes it clear God wants us to prosper. Don't let the unknown stop you from moving on through life. Keep seeking God where you doubt He is.

Write Proverbs 21:12.

_____

_____

_____

_____

_____

The secret to a prosperous life is found in loving and fearing the Lord, obeying and walking in the ways of His Word, and yielding continually to His spirit within you. That's God esteem.

The healing of shame begins when you identify and confess the lies you believe about yourself. You must begin replacing those lies with biblical truth about who God is and who you are as His child: a person of immeasurable worth, righteous, and uncondemned. He knows the things that cause you to doubt and the things that set your soul on fire. He knows how many hairs are on your head. Only God brings full emotional cleansing and freedom. In God's eyes, you are loved, cherished, seen, and adored.

> Let your conduct be without covetousness; be content with such things as you have. For He Himself has said, I will never leave you nor forsake you. (Hebrews 13:5 NKJV)

As a Christian woman reads the Bible day by day, her mind will be renewed with a new way of thinking about life.

> And He said to them, Why are you troubled? And why do doubts arise in your hearts? (Luke 24:38 NKJV)

You are not forgotten; God remembers and sees you. He sees everything about you—your failing, fears, doubts, weaknesses, insecurities, happiness, love, peace, and joy. God loves you because you are His. It doesn't matter what you can or cannot do or because of how good or bad you are. God knows and cares all about you. In God's eyes, you are valued, loved, cherished, seen, and adored.

You may doubt lots of things, but one thing you can't doubt is that God loves you. The assurance of salvation is a mighty defense against the doubt and insecurity in your thoughts.

Write a Prayer

_____

Everyone is looking for a happy and balanced life.
Write Romans 8:31.

_____

_____

_____

_____

_____

Life can be hard. Christians don't have a trouble-free life. When you turn your worries into worship, God will turn your battles into blessings. You are not alone; the Holy Spirit will help you, guide you, and teach you.

Write a Prayer

_____

_____

_____

_____

_____

_____

_____

_____

_____

Self-Control and Mindset

Merriam-Webster defines *self-control* as "the restraint exercised over one's own impulses, emotions, or desires." *Mindset* is "a mental attitude or inclination."

You are the only one who has complete control over your thoughts, emotions, actions, and behavior. You have to make a conscious effort to catch yourself before you say or do something, whether it is good or bad. You already have all the discipline you need.

> Let all things be done decently and in order.
> (1 Corinthians 14:40 KJV)

What thoughts do you need to gain control of?

_____
_____
_____
_____
_____

What emotion do you need to gain control of?

_____
_____
_____
_____
_____

What actions do you need to take control over?

_____
_____
_____
_____
_____

Have you listened to yourself lately? _____
Your words can shape other people's lives. You can't take back words once they are spoken. Try exchanging careless words that hurt with intentional words that encourage. Recognize words that tear down, and replace them with words that build up. Train your brain to help you think before you speak. Be good stewards of the words that God has given you to say. Stop being disappointed by your lack of control, and embrace the power of the Holy Spirit.

Write Titus 2:1.

_____
_____
_____
_____
_____

In overcoming problems whether physical, emotional, or spiritual admit you are in need and desire a change. Do you care enough about your problems to do something about them, even if it requires some action, effort, sacrifice or even suffering? _____

What problem needs your attention right now?

_____
_____
_____
_____
_____

How are you going to fix it?

_____

_____

_____

_____

The enemy will whisper toxic lies that this world will solve our problems, numb your pain, and bring the rewards you are looking for, by getting your focus on anything other than God, with thoughts like you're a loser, you're worthless, or you're a failure. God does not make mistakes; He doesn't make worthless losers or failures.

Write Deuteronomy 14:2.

_____

_____

_____

_____

You are created to be in a relationship with God and to live according to His word with all your heart, mind, body, and soul.

Unfulfilled dreams create emotional pain and are most often misunderstood by others. Find someone who will listen and give support, someone with a faithful spirit, is trustworthy, will provide hope, and be uplifting.

Whom can you reach out to?

_____

_____

_____

_____

Do you really want to make a change in your life? _____
You are the only one who can make the change.

Notes

_____

_____

_____

_____

_____

_____

_____

_____

_____

_____

Write a Prayer

_____

_____

_____

_____

_____

_____

_____

_____

_____

_____

Write 2 Timothy 1:7.

_____

_____

_____

_____

_____

Use meditation, exercise, healthy eating, laughter, or hobbies, anything that puts you into a positive frame of mind.

Happiness is not something you find or that other people give you. It's something you choose on your own.

Write and meditate on Psalm 28:7.

_____

_____

_____

_____

_____

Train your mind to hear what God whispers and not what the enemy may be shouting.

Give all your worries and cares to God, for
he cares for you. (1 Peter 5:7)

Why do you let your mind go there again? Do you ever make up your mind that bad things are going to happen? Are you worn out, discouraged, or desperate? God has a better plan. Let go of worry. Stop and see yourself in God's presence; experience His power and resting provision. Take your worries, and give them to God. He knows that you feel discouraged by what you can and can't control. God wants to exchange your worries for His peace and promises. Replace worry with gratitude. God is faithful, and He won't let you down.

What are you worrying about right now?

_____

_____

_____

_____

_____

Write a prayer asking God to help you.

_____

_____

_____

_____

_____

God sees everything—your mess-ups, failings, fear, weaknesses, insecurities, and doubts—and He finds value. God doesn't love you any more or less because of what you can or cannot do. He loves you because you are His, made in His image, and fashioned by His heart.

Emotions are at the core of your being, by reflecting your attitude, behavior, and will. Being able to experience pain, anger, happiness, sadness, and joy is being able to feel alive. But don't be led by your emotions. Watch your thoughts; don't entertain thoughts of negativity. Negative thoughts are more powerful than positive thoughts. Cast all your cares and negativity to Him.

Also, when you take time for self-care, you aren't being selfish. You are simply helping support your mind and body so you can be present for the people who rely on you. It's emotional first aid for your life.

Write Exodus 15:2.

_____

_____

_____

_____

_____

Until now you have not asked for anything
in my name. Ask and you will receive, and your
joy will be complete. (John 16:24 NIV)

Write a Prayer

Everyone's emotions affect their physical condition. A heart of peace helps produce a healthy body.

God's answers to your prayers are better in every way than your own. He knows what is around every corner, over every hill, and down in every valley. You have to trust Him to answer your prayers in His own timing and in His own way.

Excuses are an expression of regret for failure to do something. Recognize the excuses you use to keep you from doing something: "I'll do it later," "It doesn't matter to anyone else," "I don't have the time," "It can wait," etc. Life doesn't get in the way; you get in the way.

List the excuses you use most often.

Now own up to them, and do what you want to do regardless of what you think is holding you back. You can have results or excuses but not both.

You will feel better when you can cross things off your to-do or bucket list. It doesn't matter how big or how small the task; stop putting it off.

Spend more time with God and less time on the busyness of life.

What are you waiting to do?

_____

_____

_____

_____

_____

_____

_____

_____

Cast your burdens on the Lord and He shall
sustain you; He shall never permit the righteous
to be moved. (Psalm 55:22 NKJV)

True faith generates action. To ensure you are always in control of your life, stop making excuses. Be stronger than your excuses.
Write Hebrews 12:1.

_____

_____

_____

_____

_____

Write a Prayer

_____
_____
_____
_____
_____
_____
_____
_____
_____
_____
_____

Finding calm in the chaos is essential to weathering any storm and maintaining health and sanity.

Notes

_____
_____
_____
_____
_____
_____
_____
_____
_____

Guilt and Fear

Merriam-Webster defines *guilt* as "the feelings of deserving blame for offenses, or a feeling of responsibility or remorse for some offense, crime, wrong, etc., whether real or imagined."

Release guilt from your life. Choose gratitude over guilt. By having a relationship with God, you will transform guilt with faith and love.

Write 1 John 1:9.

_____

_____

_____

_____

_____

Guilt is the emotional and spiritual weight we bear as the result of sin against others and against God.

Let go of any guilt you have from your past. Ask God to forgive you. He wants to hear from you.

Carrying guilt for something that was done to you can weigh you down and hold you back from enjoying life. It can affect all areas of your life.

Notes

_____
_____
_____
_____
_____
_____
_____
_____
_____
_____

Write a Prayer

_____
_____
_____
_____
_____
_____
_____
_____
_____
_____

Guilt can cause fear—fear that someone will find out or remind you of the sin in your life.

Fear is a part of life. We all battle fear. Is fear stopping you from living a fulfilling life? Put fear in its place. Fear and anxiety come when you assume control instead of allowing God to be God in your life. He really is who He says He is, and He will do what He promises to do. Surrender yourself to the Father, "for God hath not given us the spirit of fear: but of power, and of love, and of a sound mind" (2 Timothy 1:7 NKJV). You learned to fear; therefore, it can be unlearned.

Write and reflect on Psalm 56:3.

_____
_____
_____
_____
_____

You will not become more courageous and learn to live boldly by avoiding your fears. Your courage is strengthened by faithfulness and love for God. You fear things you can't control and fear the things you can. God knows you will struggle.

In God I trust; I will not be afraid.

> She is clothed with strength and dignity, and she laughs without fear of the future. (Proverbs 31:25 NLT)

What are you afraid of, and what is fear keeping you from?

_____
_____
_____
_____
_____
_____
_____

Don't be afraid to enjoy life to the fullest.

> Have I not commanded you? Be strong and courageous. Do not be discouraged for the Lord your God will be with you wherever you go. (Joshua 1:9 NIV)

Write Psalm 77:1.

_____

_____

_____

_____

_____

Fear tries to derail God's plan and purpose for your lives. Rely on God as your shield. Realize that He hears and answers your prayers. Write a prayer for your biggest fear.

_____

_____

_____

_____

_____

_____

_____

_____

Do not be overcome by evil, but overcome
evil with good. (Romans 12:21 NIV)

Do you fear unimportance or worry about being dumb, weak, and worthless? God wants you to stop listening to the voices and let Him tell you your value.

Trust in the Lord with all your heart and
lean not on your own understanding; in all your
ways submit to Him and He will make your
paths straight. (Proverbs 3:5–6 NIV)

Write a Prayer

So do not fear, for I am with you; do not be dismayed, for I am your God. I will strengthen you and help you; I will uphold you with my righteous right hand. (Isaiah 41:10 NIV)

Write a Prayer

Find someone to pray for you and lift you up. God has not called you to go through life alone. All throughout the Bible, He brought people together for mutual encouragement and support.

Notes

_____

_____

_____

_____

_____

_____

_____

_____

_____

_____

_____

_____

_____

_____

Love and Joy

Love is an often overused or misused word. "I love this." "I love that." Love is not a word we say, but love is something we do. Love is an ongoing and deliberate choice, not an emotion or a feeling. Love sometimes demands that we act in very unpractical and even uncomfortable ways. We are commanded to love one another, to do acts of love, and to respond lovingly to others.

But *joy* is "a state of happiness," "a source or cause of delight." God is the only true source of love and joy.

> Pleasant words are like a honey comb, sweetness to the soul and health to the bones. (Proverbs 16:24 NKJV)

Write 1 John 3:11.

_____

_____

_____

_____

_____

> And now abide faith, hope, love, these three; but the greatest of these is love. (1 Corinthians 13:13 NKJV)

Write 1 John 4:7.

_____

_____

_____

_____

> But above all these things put on love, which
> is the bond of perfection. (Colossians 3:14 NKJV)

Write Psalm 119:159.

_____

_____

_____

_____

> You shall love the Lord your God with all
> your heart, with all your soul, and with all your
> strength. (Deuteronomy 6:5 NKJV)

Write John 13:34.

_____

_____

_____

_____

A prosperous life is found in loving the Lord, obeying and walking in His Word and to His spirit within you. God wants you to love in such a way that people around you will know you are a follower of Christ. He wants you to love others in the same way He loves you.

Write a Prayer

_____
_____
_____
_____
_____
_____
_____
_____
_____
_____
_____
_____

Look around, and be in awe that the God of the universe, who created everything in your view, also created you. Take the time to enjoy something you love and that makes you smile.

Joy increases as believers become more intimate in their fellowship with God.

My lips shout for joy when I sing praise to You,
I whom you have delivered. (Psalm 71:23 NIV)

What is something that truly brings you joy?

_____
_____
_____
_____
_____

Write Psalm 51:12.

_____
_____
_____
_____
_____

Now may the God of hope fill you with
all joy and peace in believing, that you may
abound in hope by the power of the Holy Spirit.
(Romans 15:13 NKJV)

Happiness is a feeling of spiritual contentment that will carry
you through the triumphs, trials, and heartaches of life with calm sta-
bility, serenity, peace, and tranquility. Happiness is a positive choice,
when a believer's faith and conduct are balanced. Happiness comes
from daily obedience and faith in the Lord.

And we know that all things work together
for good to those who love God, to those who
are the called according to His purpose. (Romans
8:28 NKJV)

Write Romans 14:17.

_____
_____
_____
_____
_____

The Lord is my strength and my shield; my
heart trusts in Him, and He helps me. My heart
leaps for joy, and with my song I praise Him.
(Psalm 28:7 NKJV)

Write John 15:11.

_____

_____

_____

_____

_____

> Rejoice in the Lord always. I will say it again: Rejoice. (Philippians 4:4 NIV)

> Indeed, you are our glory and joy. (1 Thessalonians 2:20 NIV)

Write 1 Thessalonians 5:16.

_____

_____

_____

_____

_____

Write Psalm 118:24.

_____

_____

_____

_____

_____

God cares for and knows all about you. Love yourself as much as you love your children or your spouse. The love you give has to be authentic and pure.

Where do you find peace?

_____
_____
_____
_____
_____

Write a Prayer

_____
_____
_____
_____
_____
_____
_____
_____
_____

Until now you have not asked for anything
in my name. Ask and you will receive and your
joy will be complete. (John 16:24 NIV)

Happiness is a pleasant mental state, but joy is a pleasant spiritual state.

Remember, true love is God love.

Praise the Lord! Oh give thanks to the Lord,
for He is good, for His steadfast love endures forever! (Psalm 106:1 ESV)

Notes

_____
_____
_____
_____
_____
_____
_____
_____
_____
_____
_____
_____
_____
_____

Peer Pressure and Freedom

Peer pressure, or worldly pressure, is a feeling that one must do the same things as other people of the same age and social group do to be liked or respected. Our freedom, whether political or spiritual, depends on God's initiative of freedom from sin's curse.

You are running your own race. No need to jump on someone's bandwagon. Everyone has their own opinions, roles, and personalities, and it's important to remember you can't control anyone else.

Do not believe everything you hear or read in the news or on social media. Satan is everywhere and will cause people to go astray.

Stop judging by mere appearances, but instead judge correctly. All believers are one in Christ. (John 7:24 NIV)

Communication and shared fellowship are the greatest weapons against prejudice.

For God does not show favoritism. (Romans 2:11 NIV)

God disapproves of all mistreatment according to race. The Bible does not say that one race is superior to another. Would God be pleased with the way you treat those of another race? Worldly ideas, attitudes, and prejudices must be replaced by thoughts that conform to God's ways.

> He did not discriminate between us and
> them, for He purified their hearts by faith. (Acts
> 15:9 NIV)

Unfaithfulness creeps into lives when hearts are more closely attuned to contemporary culture and peer pressure than they are to the voice of God.

A genuine relationship with Christ will be evident in the personal relationships you have with others.

Write James 2:8.

_____
_____
_____
_____
_____

> Do everything without grumbling or argu-
> ing, so that you may become blameless and pure,
> children of God without fault in a warped and
> crooked generation. (Philippians 2:14–15 NIV)

Taking a stand for everything Christ-like should make you happy and feel good. One person can make a difference.

As a Christian, you should not be a customer of any company that supports organizations or groups that go against God's teachings. Yes, that can be hard in some cases, but how do you feel about it?

Write John 3:16.

_____
_____
_____
_____
_____

Write a Prayer

_____

_____

_____

_____

_____

_____

_____

_____

_____

_____

We fight with weapons that are different from those the world uses. Our weapons have power from God that can destroy the enemy's strong places. We destroy people's arguments and every proud thing that raises itself against the knowledge of God. We capture every thought and make it give up and obey Christ. (2 Corinthians 10:4–5 ICB)

How good and pleasant it is when God's people live together in unity. (Psalm 133:1 NIV)

Living in unity doesn't mean there won't be differences.

All who rage against you will surely be ashamed and disgraced; those who oppose you will be nothing and perish. (Isaiah 41:11 NIV)

And you shall know the truth, and the truth shall make you free. (John 8:32 NKJV)

You are free to believe and feel the way you want to. Do not let anyone force you to say or do something you don't believe in.

Therefore if the Son makes you free, you
shall be free indeed. (John 8:36 NKJV)

To truly feel free, stop caring about what people think. Everyone is free to have and speak their opinion. Just as you are. Doesn't mean you have to confront, react, or reply to the comments or actions of others.

Write 2 Corinthians 3:17.

_____

_____

_____

_____

_____

What's on your mind?

_____

_____

_____

_____

_____

God is preparing you; trust His plan, not your pain.

Therefore there is now no condemna-
tion for those who are in Christ Jesus, because
through Christ Jesus the law of the Spirit who
gives life has set you free from law of sin and
death. (Romans 8:1–2 NIV)

Write a Prayer

_____
_____
_____
_____
_____
_____
_____
_____
_____
_____

Be careful not to allow your freedoms cause a person of weaker faith to stumble.

You are always influencing somebody.

Live as free people, but do not use your freedom as a cover-up for evil; live as God's slaves. Show proper respect to everyone, love the family of believers fear God, honor the emperor. (1 Peter 2:16 NIV)

For kingship belongs to the Lord, and he rules over the nations. (Psalm 22:28 ESV)

Notes

_____
_____
_____
_____
_____
_____
_____

Anger and Forgiveness

Anger is an emotional response to a perceived wrong or injustice. Don't let anger build up; it eats away at your soul and can steal your joy. Anger starts with frustration. Uncontrolled frustration grows into heated arguments, outbursts, accusations, manipulations, or worse.

Anger affects everyone around you. Undisciplined anger can destroy our lives.

Anger denies the power of God to care for your needs and can even completely take over your life.

There will be times when you can't understand what's going on and will want to doubt and question God. God welcomes your anger at Him. He knows it will draw you closer to Him. He will use the pain and anger to bless you in ways that you can't imagine. Leave your anger at the feet of Jesus, and allow Him to act on your behalf.

Write Romans 12:19.

_____

_____

_____

_____

_____

What are you angry about right now?

_____

_____

_____

_____

Pray and turn all the things and people that frustrate you to God. Pray now.

_____
_____
_____
_____
_____

Do you act or react? _____
A woman who acts knows who she is, what she believes in, and how she should behave. Another person's actions do not dictate her reactions. A wise woman controls her temper rather than being controlled by it. We can't always control our circumstances, but we do have a choice as to how we react to them.
Write Ephesians 4:31 (CEV).

_____
_____
_____
_____
_____

Write a Prayer

_____
_____
_____
_____
_____
_____
_____
_____
_____

> In your anger do not sin; do not let the sun
> go down while you are still angry. (Ephesians
> 4:26 NIV)

Anger is destructive. The worst thing you can bring to any dispute is anger. It's not so much what you say, but the way you say it.

> Do not be quickly provoked in your spirit,
> for anger resides in the laps of fools. (Ecclesiastes
> 7:9 NIV)

Write Colossians 3:8.

_____

_____

_____

_____

_____

> My dear brothers and sisters, take note of
> this: everyone should be quick to listen, slow to
> speak and slow to become angry, because human
> anger does not produce the righteousness that
> God desires. (James 1:19–20 NIV)

When you're hurt or upset, you usually fail to communicate all your true feelings to the person you're upset with. Do not use words that cast blame. A forgiving spirit brings good to yourself and to others. A forgiving attitude does not excuse the self, defend the self, or accuse another.

God's forgiveness is complete, everlasting, and always available. Forgiveness comes with the removal of past offenses from the mind, followed by meditation upon scripture, giving God our hurts, and praying for the offender.

Write Matthew 6:14–15.

_____

_____

_____

_____

_____

God gives love and forgiveness over and over. Seek forgiveness from God and others, and turn away from the past mistakes to move with joyful purpose. Love is the prime ingredient in forgiveness.

Broken hearts and bruised hopes heal in the hands of Jesus. Showing mercy with a forgiving spirit brings blessings from God and gratitude from the one forgiven.

Write Ephesians 4:32.

_____

_____

_____

_____

_____

Now may the Lord of peace Himself give you peace always in every way. The Lord be with you all. (2 Timothy 3:16 NKJV)

Write 2 Chronicles 7:14.

_____

_____

_____

_____

_____

God's power is enough to deliver you from despair. Much of your suffering is rooted either in relationships or in circumstances beyond your control.

Stop apologizing for things you don't have control over. Find acceptance in the light of His love.

If there is someone to make amends with, then do so. If the other person doesn't accept your apology, then pray for them, and then it is between them and God. By doing this, you have followed Jesus's lead and let it go. When the thoughts about the situation come up, remind yourself it's been settled.

Notes

_____

_____

_____

_____

_____

_____

_____

_____

_____

Write a Prayer

_____

_____

_____

_____

_____

_____

_____

_____

_____

Write Colossians 1:13–14.

_____

_____

_____

_____

_____

Therefore, if anyone is in Christ, he is a new
creation; old things have passed away; behold, all
things have become new. (2 Corinthians 5:17)

What would your relationships look like if you love others the
way Jesus loves you?

Thoughts

_____

_____

_____

_____

_____

_____

_____

_____

_____

_____

_____

_____

_____

_____

_____

_____

_____

Faith and Gratitude

Faith is the belief and trust in and loyalty to God. It is impossible to have a full and complete life without faith. Our faith starts and ends with Jesus.

Your faith walk is different from that of everyone else. Your faith is very personal. Having faith helps you through difficult times. Faith is an invisible shield that deflects all false accusations.

> Now faith is confidence in what we hope for and assurance about what we do not see. Therefore our faith, our confidence, our assurance and our hope are grounded in the sovereignty of God. (Hebrews 11:1 NIV)

Write Hebrews 11:4.

_____
_____
_____
_____
_____

God is in control. You are to love Him and pursue His purpose. God went out of His way to teach and love.

> And we know that God causes everything to work together for the good of those who love God and are called according to His purpose for them. (Romans 8:28 NLT)

To find hope in a time of crisis establish a daily routine with God and trust God's sovereignty.

What crisis are you having today?

_____
_____
_____
_____
_____

God's got this. He is in charge, He is in control, and He loves you. Our hope is in Him. He made you, and He knows how to fix what is broken within you. Act upon what God tells you to do. When you need help, God will send Jesus in the form of a person, a verse from His word, a podcast, or in a thought.

I will cry out to God Most High, to God who
performs all things for me. (Psalm 57:2 NKJV)

Notes

_____
_____
_____
_____
_____
_____
_____
_____
_____

Write Psalm 35:19–20.

God promises to hear and to answer the prayers of all who seek forgiveness and who ask in faith. God's answers include yes, no, and maybe. He promises to answer the sincere intent of the heart, even if you cannot find the right words. Pray in faith.

Write Jeremiah 33:3.

Praying opens the channels between you and God. Your faith is fueled by your focus.

What are you focusing on?

Be joyful in hope, patient in affliction,
faithful in prayer. (Romans 12:12 NIV)

Write John 14:6.

_____
_____
_____
_____
_____

> Ask and it will be given to you; seek and you will find; knock and the door will be opened to you. (Matthew 7:7 NIV)

Write Hebrews 11:40.

_____
_____
_____
_____
_____

Obedience is the one condition you must meet to experience a blessing from God, and you want every blessing God has for you.

Write a Prayer

_____
_____
_____
_____
_____
_____
_____
_____
_____

No temptation has overtaken you except what is common to mankind. And God is faithful; he will not let you be tempted beyond what you can bear. But, when you are tempted, he will also provide a way out so that you can endure it. (1 Corinthians 10: 13 NIV)

What kind of faith do you have?

_____

_____

_____

_____

_____

Use your trials and tribulations to endure, persevere, and become spiritually mature so that you can experience joy.
Write Psalm 56:3.

_____

_____

_____

_____

_____

For we walk by faith, not by sight. (2 Corinthians 5:7 NKJV)

Gratitude, or being thankful, is important for a healthy lifestyle, by focusing on all that God has blessed you with.

The Lord your God in your midst, The Mighty One, will save; He will rejoice over you with gladness, He will quiet you with His love, He will rejoice over you singing. (Zephaniah 3:17 NKJV)

The blessings of God are abundantly bestowed on all those who follow Him. Life's blessings are not a measure of who you are, but of who God is. God promises personal blessings to those who follow Him in obedience and exhorts His people to be a blessing to others. God promises continual blessings on earth and eternal blessings in heaven.

Believers praise God in all things. Genuine praise will flow from your heart even during times of sorrow, discouragement, trial, and temptation. Praise God wherever you are. Praise God all the time.

Write Philippians 4:6.

_____

_____

_____

_____

_____

List five ways to bless someone today.

_____

_____

_____

_____

_____

Be comfortable with what God has given you.

Notes

_____
_____
_____
_____
_____
_____
_____
_____
_____
_____

Write a Prayer

_____
_____
_____
_____
_____
_____
_____
_____
_____
_____

Real praise is not half-hearted; it involves your whole heart.

I will give thanks to the Lord because of His righteousness; I will sing the praises of the name of the Lord Most High. (Psalm 7:17 NIV)

I will give thanks to You, Lord, with all my heart; I will tell of all Your wonderful deeds. (Psalm 9:1 NIV)

God is always listening.

Notes

_____
_____
_____
_____
_____
_____
_____
_____
_____

How has your journey shaped you so far?

_____
_____
_____
_____

What will you do to plan for the journey ahead?

_____
_____
_____
_____
_____

About the Author

Christie is a Christian, a wife, a mother, and a grandmother in South Arkansas. She is also a cracked pot in the Potter's hand, with a hope to lead others to Christ, strengthen faith, and find joy with a change in mindset.

CPSIA information can be obtained
at www.ICGtesting.com
Printed in the USA
LVHW030240040322
712524LV00001BB/175